CRANKS
PUDDINGS & DESSERTS

Compiled by Daphne Swann

To our customers worldwide

Cranks is indebted to the following people whose help in producing this book has been invaluable.

Jane Suthering and Val Fisher, who between them adapted, devised and tested the recipes in this book with great expertise and unfailing enthusiasm.

Jane Lydbury, illustrator.

Grant Symon, photographer.

Karen Boxell helped by Gail Moore, our two secretaries, for their patience, good humour and skills in the endless checking, collating and typing of this book.

Published in Great Britain by Guinness Superlatives Ltd,
33 London Road, Enfield, Middlesex, England.

Designed by Newell and Sorrell, 14 Utopia Village, Chalcot Road, London NW1 8LH.

Cranks deserts & puddings.
1. Deserts   2. Cookery (Natural foods)
I. Cranks Limited
641.8'6   TX773

ISBN 0–85112–881–5

Printed in Italy by Arnoldo Mondadori Editore, Vicenza

INTRODUCTION

When Cranks opened its first restaurant 25 years ago (in Carnaby Street in London's Soho) its name exactly reflected how most people viewed wholefood and vegetarian restaurants – nutty in more senses than one! Now, of course, the lonely furrow that Cranks then ploughed has become the broad highway for a great many.

From the very beginning Cranks became something of a cult and throughout has remained the benchmark by which all other similar enterprizes have to be judged. Not only has there been an unswerving commitment to wholefood and vegetarian food without additives or preservatives (to this day Cranks still use flour from Pimhill Farm in Shropshire, which was one of the first to become totally organic) but there has also been a vigorous experimentation, innovation and creation of new dishes. And although now the food served at any of Cranks expanding family of restaurants is sophisticated by comparison with the relatively simple fare of the earliest days, there still remains a satisfying practicality and unfussiness in the recipes which is a refreshing change from the pretentiousness of many restaurants and cookbooks.

The continual creation of new dishes has, over the years, produced a vast number of tried and tested recipes – and it's from this repertoire of new dishes that the very best have been selected for inclusion in this series of handy little books.

NOTES ON
INGREDIENTS

Agar The vegetarian substitute for gelatine.
It is derived from a sea vegetable and produces a
slightly cloudy jelly when set. It is available as a powder
or in flakes.

Arrowroot Used as a thickening agent, this white
powder extracted from the rhizome of a herbacious
plant from the West Indies is believed to be helpful with
digestive disorders.

Apple Concentrate This syrupy brown concentrated
apple juice is available in bottles in most health food
shops.

Butter Cranks recommend using an unsalted butter.
Vegetarian margarine may, of course, be substituted in
all recipes where butter is stated.

Carob The ideal substitute for chocolate. It is made from
the ground fruit of the carob tree. Available ground in
powder form or as a bar which can be grated, melted
down or simply eaten like chocolate. It is rich in
vitamins, contains no refined sugar or caffeine.
Available in most health food shops.

Citrus Fruits Thoroughly wash all citrus fruit rinds
before using to remove any chemical deposits. Better
still, use organically grown fruit.

Coconut Can be bought in various forms – desiccated or
shredded which is finely grated and dried, or creamed.
This is sold in bars or tubs and can be broken off and
melted for use in cooking. Coconut milk powder is sold

4

like dried milk. All can be found in good health food or oriental shops.

Coffee Decaffeinated coffee either beans, ground, or instant is now readily available. Look out for the water extraction method which is generally recognised as being a better method of decaffeinating.

Eggs Cranks only uses free-range eggs in its bakeries and therefore recommend them in all the recipes. Many free range eggs are not graded but as a guideline we would use size 3. They are now readily available in most shops – do be sure to look for the label "free range".

Flour Cranks uses 100% wholemeal stoneground and organically grown flour in all recipes – thus using the whole of the wheat berry. White flour has all the valuable bran and germ removed. *Buckwheat* flour is ground buckwheat made from the seeds of the plant known as Saracen corn. It has a distinctive flavour and is ideal for pancakes.

Freezing Recipes which are suitable for freezing will be marked by asterisks (***).

Jam Some excellent sugar-free jams are now available. Once opened they should be refrigerated. Alternatively Cranks recommends unrefined sugar jams – some are now made with organically grown fruit with no additives or preservatives.

Nutter A pure white vegetable fat made from nut oils, the vegetarian alternative to lard.

Oil Sunflower, safflower and soya oil are all good to use in cooking being mild in flavour and low in saturated fats.

Sugar Unrefined brown sugar is used in all Cranks recipes. It is free from artificial colourings and other additives and is available in five types – Demerara, light muscovado, muscovado, molasses and golden granulated. For authenticity check the packet for the country of origin, usually Mauritius.

Tahini A thick oily paste made from roasted sesame seeds and rich in fat, protein, minerals – may be thinned down with water.

Tofu A soya bean curd with a soft delicate texture and pale colour. Sold in slabs or slices, available plain, with herbs, smoked or marinated. It should be kept refrigerated. The softer consistency is called silken tofu.

Trail mix A mixture of sliced nuts, chopped dried fruits and seeds available from health food shops.

Yoghourt Whole or skimmed milk is injected with a live bacteria and left to ferment to produce yoghourt. It is a good form of protein, low in fat if made with skimmed milk and a good source of calcium. Greek strained yoghourt is creamy and smoother than ordinary yoghourt and is an excellent substitute for cream.

WHOLE MEAL PASTRY CHART
easy guide to quantities

100% wholemeal flour	baking powder	½ butter ½ Nutter	water (approx)
4oz (100g)	1 tsp (5ml)	2oz (50 g)	4 tsp (20 ml)
5oz (150 g)	1½ tsp (7.5 ml)	2½oz (75g)	2 tbsp (30 ml)
6oz (175g)	1½ tsp (7.5 ml)	3oz (85 g)	2 tbsp (30 ml)
7oz (200 g)	2 tsp (10 ml)	3½ oz (100 g)	3 tbsp (45 ml)
9oz (250 g)	2½ tsp (12.5ml)	4½oz (125 g)	4 tbsp (60 ml)
10oz (300 g)	1 tbsp (15 ml)	5oz (150 g)	4 tbsp (60 ml)
12oz (350 g)	3 tbsp (15 ml)	6oz (175 g)	5 tbsp (75 ml)
14oz (400 g)	4 tbsp (20 ml)	7oz (200 g)	5 tbsp (75 ml)

Put the flour and baking powder into a basin. Rub in the fat until the mixture resembles fine crumbs. Add sufficient warm water to give a soft but manageable dough. Cover with cling film and leave at room temperature until ready to use.

US EQUIVALENTS

An American pint measures 16 fl oz (500 ml) and there are 2 cups (8 fl oz (250 ml) each) to the pint. The British pint is 20 fl oz (600 ml).

British Standard measuring spoons are:
1 teaspoon = 5 ml
1 tablespoon = 15 ml
Hence there are 3 teaspoons to one tablespoon.
An American tablespoon is 4 teaspoons (20 ml)

There is no easy guide for translating recipes from English to American but here are a few standard amounts.
1 cup butter = 8 oz (225 g)
1 cup sugar = 7 oz (200 g)
1 cup flour = 5 oz (150 g)

PUDDINGS & DESSERTS

In this book we have chosen a varying range of sweets for all occasions – there are pies and open fruit flans, sponge puddings and crumbles, mousses, delicious fresh fruit ice creams, parfaits and sorbets and a variety of fruit salads. We have included some alternative suggestions for Christmas and some stunning gateaux for parties, all prepared with 100% wholemeal flour, free-range eggs, unrefined sugar and carob. (If you haven't tried carob, it's a delicious look-a-like alternative to chocolate with a distinctive flavour of its own and has the added advantage of being caffeine-free). There are one or two rich and very special desserts like the chilled Mocha Brandy Slice, the Carob Truffle Gateau or Sherried Syllabub Trifle, but to balance these indulgences, there are some simple fruit recipes refreshing and ideal to round off a sustaining meal.

Colour and presentation plays an important part in the enjoyment of preparing desserts – try to use fresh herb sprigs and edible flowers and leaves to decorate, being careful not to overdo it – just one sprig of mint or finely sliced kiwi fruit or a twist of lime can finish a dish perfectly.

RICH WHOLEMEAL SHORTCRUST PASTRY

Butter 3 oz (75 g)
Wholemeal flour 4½ oz (115 g)
Unrefiend brown sugar 1 oz (25 g)
Iced water 1 tbsp (15 ml)

Rub the butter into the flour until the mixture resembles fine crumbs. Stir in the sugar and mix to a firm dough with the measured water.

***

MACAROONS

Egg white 1
Ground almonds 2 oz (50 g)
Unrefined brown sugar, sifted 3 oz (75 g)
Almond essence, optional ½ tsp (2.5 ml)
Flaked almonds 1 tbsp (15 ml) or whole almonds 12

Line a baking sheet with rice paper or non-stick paper. Whisk the egg white until stiff, then fold in the ground almonds, sugar and almond essence. Spoon or pipe (using a ½ inch (1.5 cm) plain nozzle) 12 macaroons.

Top each with flaked almonds or a whole almond. Bake at 180°C /350°F/gas mark 4 for about 20 minutes. Cool on the tray, then carefully remove to a wire tray and leave to go cold.

Trim the rice paper from around each biscuit, if using.

Makes 12
***

WHOLEMEAL SPONGE FINGERS

Free-range eggs 3
Unrefined brown sugar 3 oz (75 g)
Vanilla essence ¼ tsp (1.25 ml)
Wholemeal flour 4 oz (100 g)

Put the eggs, sugar and vanilla essence in a bowl over a saucepan of simmering water and whisk until very thick and pale (the whisk should leave a strong trail in the mixture). Remove from the heat and carefully fold in the flour. Spoon the mixture into a piping bag fitted with a ½ in (1.5 cm) plain nozzle and pipe finger lengths approx. 4 in (10 cm) of sponge mixture onto greased baking trays, allowing room for spreading. Bake at 375°F/190°C/gas mark 5 for 5–7 minutes until just firm to the touch. Cool on a wire tray.

Makes 30–35
***

WHOLEMEAL SPONGE CAKE

Butter or margarine 4 oz (100 g)
Unrefined brown sugar 4 oz (100 g)
Free-range eggs, beaten 3
Self-raising wholemeal flour 4 oz (100 g)

Grease and base line two 7 in (18 cm) sandwich tins. Cream the butter and sugar until pale and fluffy. Beat in the eggs a little at a time. Fold in the flour. Divide the mixture evenly between the prepared tins. Level the surface and bake at 350°F/180°C/gas mark 4 for about 15 minutes until risen and firm to the touch. Cool on a wire tray. Alternatively, bake in one 8 in (20 cm) cake tin for 25–30 minutes.

Makes about 1 lb (450 g)
***

DARK GINGERCAKE

Wholemeal flour 6 oz (175 g)
Ground ginger 2 tsp (10 ml)
Ground mixed spice 1 tsp (5 ml)
Bicarbonate of soda ½ tsp (2.5 ml)
Molasses 6 oz (175 g)
Unrefined brown sugar 1½ oz (40 g)
Butter 3 oz (75 g)
Free-range eggs, beaten 2
Milk 4 fl oz (100 ml)

Grease and base line a 7 in (18 cm) cake tin. Mix together the flour, ginger, mixed spice and bicarbonate of soda in a large bowl.

Warm together the molasses, sugar and butter until melted, and add to the dry ingredients with the eggs and milk. Beat well until evenly mixed, then transfer to the prepared tin. Bake at 325°F/170°C/gas mark 3 for about 1 hour until risen and firm to the touch. Cool slightly, remove from the tin and transfer to a wire tray to go cold.

Makes about 1 lb 6 oz (625 g)
***

BUCKWHEAT PANCAKES

Serve these pancakes hot with Cashew & Apple Sauce
(p. 13) or fresh lemon juice and honey. A dollop of
double cream or strained Greek yoghourt makes it
extra delicious.

Buckwheat flour 2 oz (50 g)
Free-range egg 1
Milk or water ¼ pt (150 ml)
Oil 2 tbsp (30 ml)
Oil or melted butter for frying

Combine the ingredients for the pancakes and blend in
a liquidizer or food processor to give a pouring batter,
adding a little extra liquid if necessary. Alternatively
place the flour in a basin. Add the egg and slowly beat
in the milk and oil. Heat a little oil or butter in a 6 in
(15 cm) frying pan and pour in about 3 tbsp of mixture.
Swirl quickly to cover the base of the pan and cook until
golden. Turn the pancake and cook the other side until
golden. Continue until all the mixture is used up.

Makes 8
***

CUSTARD SAUCE

A traditional sauce made with our special ingredients to serve with a variety of puddings and fruit dishes.

Milk ½ pt (300 ml)
Egg yolks 3
Unrefined brown sugar 1 tbsp (15 ml)
Arrowroot 1 tsp (5 ml)
Vanilla essence ¼tsp (1.25 ml)

Heat the milk until it almost boils. Beat the egg yolks, sugar, arrowroot and vanilla essence together. Add the hot milk and stir until combined then strain it back into the saucepan and stir over the heat until the sauce thickens. Remove from the heat immediately.

CASHEW & APPLE SAUCE

A useful sauce to serve with any pudding – and it's suitable for vegans. We use it with buckwheat pancakes.

Broken cashews 4 oz (100 g)
Apple concentrate 2 tbsp (30 ml) (see p. 4)
Iced water ¼ pt (150 ml)

Place all the ingredients in a liquidizer and blend until smooth. Add extra water, if necessary, to thin down the sauce.

Makes 8 fl oz (250 ml).

CRANKS FRUIT MINCEMEAT

Cooking apple, cored and
finely chopped 4 oz (100 g)
Nutter 1 oz (25g) (see p. 5)
Raisins 3 oz (75 g)
Sultanas 3 oz (75 g)
Currants 3 oz (75 g)
Unrefined brown sugar 2 oz (50 g)
Ground cinnamon ¼ tsp (1.25 ml)
Ground nutmeg ¼ tsp (1.25 ml)
Ground mixed spice ¼ tsp (1.25 ml)
Orange, grated rind & juice of ½
Lemon, grated rind & juice of ½
Flaked almonds ½ oz (15 g)
Brandy 1–2 tbsp (15–30 ml)

Put all the ingredients, except the almonds and brandy, into a deep ovenproof dish and mix together thoroughly. Cover with a lid or foil and bake in the oven at 250°F/120°C/gas mark ½ for 1 hour. Give the mincemeat a good stir halfway through the cooking time. Leave to cool before adding the almonds and brandy. Keep refrigerated.

***

FRESH FRUIT MUESLI

This recipe is not to be confused with breakfast muesli
cereal. It will keep in the fridge for several days.

Jumbo oats 4 tbsp (60 ml)
Milk, warmed 4 fl oz (100 ml)
Thick set yoghourt ¼ pt (150 ml)
Honey 4 tbsp (60 ml)
Eating apples, grated 2
Fresh berries such as raspberries,
blackberries, strawberries, blueberries 8 oz (225 g)
Hazelnuts, chopped 4 tbsp (60 ml)
Extra berries and sprigs of
lemon balm or scented geranium to decorate

Soak the oats in the milk for 15 minutes. Mix in
yoghourt and honey.

Just before serving fold in fruit and nuts until just
mixed. Serve in individual dishes decorated with extra
berries and lemon balm or scented geranium.

Serves 4

ORANGE & STRAWBERRY TERRINE

A simple yet sophisticated jelly. Make on day of serving.

Small strawberries 6-8 oz (175-225 g)
Large oranges 4
Freshly squeezed orange juice 18 fl oz (500 ml)
Agar flakes 4 tbsp (60 ml) (see p. 4)
Strawberries and strawberry leaves to decorate

Wash and hull the strawberries. Peel the oranges using a small serrated knife to remove all the white pith. Remove the segments carefully from the central membrane. Squeeze out any juice from the peelings. Place the measured orange juice in a saucepan with the agar flakes. Bring slowly to the boil, then simmer for 3 minutes. Leave to cool. Arrange half the orange segments over the base of a 1 lb (450 g) loaf tin. Cover with orange juice. Chill until set. Make a layer of strawberries, then cover with orange juice. Chill until set. Repeat the orange layer once more, then chill until required. Unmould onto a plate and cut into thick slices to serve. Decorate with strawberries and leaves.

Serves 6

PUREED APPLE JELLY

Agar flakes are used as the setting agent for this apple jelly.

Cooking apples 1 lb (450 g)
Water ¼ pt (150 ml)
Unrefined brown sugar 3 oz (75 g)
Agar flakes 2 tbsp (30 ml) (see p. 4)
Trail mix (see p. 7) or dried fruit,
or almonds, chopped 2 oz (50 g)
Fresh cream to serve

Wash and roughly chop the apples. Place in a saucepan with the water. Cover and simmer for about 15 minutes to a pulp. Sieve the apples and return the purée to a clean pan. Stir in the sugar and then agar flakes. Bring to the boil, stirring, and simmer for 2–3 minutes. Stir in the trail mix, fruit or nuts, as wished, and transfer the mixture to a 1¼ pt (750 ml) wetted mould or pudding basin. Chill for several hours until set. Unmould and serve with fresh cream.

Serves 4

YELLOW FRUIT SALAD

A combination of tropical fruits in a lightly spiced fruit
syrup.

White grape juice ¼ pt (150 ml)
Honey 2 tbsp (30 ml)
Cardamom seeds, crushed 24
Paw paw 1
Mango 1
Medium pineapple ½
Medium melon ½
Peaches or nectarines 2
Lime, juice of ½

Place the grape juice, honey and cardamom seeds in a
saucepan. Simmer gently, covered, for 5 minutes.
Leave to go cold. Prepare all the fruits and cut into bite-
sized pieces. Place in a fruit bowl and sprinkle with lime
juice. Strain the syrup over, toss carefully and chill
lightly.

Serves 6–8

RED FRUIT COMPOTE

Rhubarb 1 lb (450 g)
Unrefined brown sugar 3 oz (75 g)
Water ¼ pt (150 ml)
Red fruits to include
raspberries, strawberries and redcurrants 8 oz (225 g)

Trim and cut the rhubarb into 1 in (2.5 cm) lengths.
Dissolve the sugar in the water and carefully poach the
rhubarb for about 10 minutes until just tender. Remove
from the heat and leave to go cold. Prepare the red
berries, as necessary, and stir gently into the rhubarb
being careful not to break the fruits.

Serves 4

CHESTNUT, APRICOT & ORANGE COMPOTE

A well-balanced combination of flavours and textures.
Delicious served with Cranks flapjacks.

Dried chestnuts 3 oz (75 g)
Dried whole apricots 6 oz (175 g)
Water ½ pt (300 ml)
Unrefined brown sugar 2 oz (50 g)
Red wine ½ pt (300 ml)
Large oranges 2

Cover the dried chestnuts with water, bring to the boil, then leave to soak for at least 12 hours. Cover the apricots with cold water and leave to soak.

Drain the chestnuts, then simmer them in the measured water for 30 minutes. Add the sugar and red wine and simmer for a further 30 minutes, or until the chestnuts are tender. Bring to the boil and cook rapidly until the liquid is reduced to about 6 fl oz (175 ml). Transfer to a bowl, drain the apricots and add to the chestnuts. Leave to cool.

Pare the rind from one orange and cut into very thin strips. Cut away the peel and white pith from the oranges, then carefully remove the segments from the inner membrane. Add the orange segments and strips of rind to the chestnuts and apricots. Squeeze the juice from the peelings and add. Stir well, cover and leave to marinate for at least 1 hour. Serve with strained Greek yoghourt or whipped cream.

Serves 4

POACHED PEARS IN
WHITE WINE

Wine and whole spices add an unusual flavour to the
poaching liquid. Delicious served with Bramble sauce
(see p. 21)

Medium-sized pears 6
White wine ½ pt (300 ml)
Water ½ pt (300 ml)
Unrefined brown sugar 2 oz (50 g)
Coriander seeds 1 tbsp (15 ml)
Whole cloves 6
Cinnamon stick 1
Lemon juice 1 tbsp (15 ml)

Carefully peel the pears leaving the stalks intact. Cut a
small slice from the base of each pear so that it will
stand up. Using a small sharp knife and starting from
the base, remove the core from each pear. Place the
pears in a saucepan with the remaining ingredients.
Bring slowly to the boil, reduce heat, cover and simmer
for about 30 minutes until the pears are tender. Remove
the pears from the pan and place in a bowl. Boil the
syrup rapidly to reduce to about 6 fl oz (175 ml). Strain
over the pears and chill until required.

Serves 6

BROWN SUGAR MERINGUES WITH BRAMBLE SAUCE

Cranks introduced unrefined sugar meringues many years ago – they are a great favourite and very delicious – especially served with a piquant fresh fruit sauce.

Egg whites 2
Unrefined brown sugar, sieved 4 oz (100 g)
Double cream, whipped ¼ pt (150 ml)

Line a baking tray with non-stick paper. Stiffly whisk the egg whites, then whisk in the sugar a spoonful at a time until really thick. Pipe or spoon 8–12 meringues on to the baking sheet. Bake at 130°C/250°F/gas mark ½ for 1½-2 hours depending on size until crisp and dry. Leave to go cold. Just before serving, sandwich together with whipped cream.

BRAMBLE SAUCE
Blackberries 12 oz (350 g)
Unrefined brown sugar 2 oz (50 g)
Arrowroot 1 tsp (5 ml)

Cook the blackberries and sugar together gently until softened. Sieve, if wished, to remove the seeds. Whisk in the arrowroot and cook over gentle heat, stirring until thickened.

Serves 4–6

DATE, COCONUT & BANANA SNOW

A sugar-free dessert relying on the natural sweetness of the fruit.

Dates, chopped 4 oz (100 g)
Creamed coconut 2 oz (50 g)
Water ¼ pt (150 ml)
Bananas, mashed 2
Egg white 1
Toasted coconut shreds to decorate

Place the dates, coconut and water in a saucepan and simmer gently until the dates have softened and the coconut melted. Leave to go cold, then stir in the banana. Stiffly whisk the egg white and fold into the mixture. Transfer to individual dishes and sprinkle with coconut. Serve at once.

Serves 4

CREAMED CHEESE WITH FRUIT

A very quick and simple dessert.

Cottage cheese 8 oz (225 g)
Honey 3 tbsp (45 ml)
Lemon, grated rind 1 tsp (5 ml)
Double cream 8 fl oz (250 ml)
Fresh fruit such as strawberries, raspberries, grapes, kiwi fruit, peaches

Push the cheese through a sieve or blend until smooth in a food processor. Beat in the honey and lemon rind. Fold in the lightly whipped cream. Pile onto a serving dish or individual dishes. Decorate with the fresh fruit.

Serves 4

AUTUMN PUDDING

A seasonal change from summer pudding using our
own sponge fingers and autumn fruits.

Wholemeal sponge fingers (approx) 30 (see p. 10)
A selection of fruit to include gooseberries, blackcurrants,
plums, blackberries, cranberries, grapes 2 lb (900 g)
Unrefined brown sugar 3 oz (75 g)
Agar flakes 1 tbsp (15 ml) (see p. 4)
Extra fruit or scented geranium leaves to decorate

Use about 24 of the sponge fingers to line the base and
sides of a 2 pt (1.2 l) pudding basin or mould, cutting
and fitting as required. Reserve any trimmings. Place
the fruits in a saucepan with the sugar and agar flakes
and simmer gently until tender, about 10 minutes. Cool
slightly then spoon into the sponge lined dish. Top
with any reserved sponge fingers and trimming and
cover with a circle of greaseproof paper. Weight down
and chill overnight. Unmould onto a serving plate.
Decorate with extra fruit or scented geranium leaves.

Serves 6
***

AVOCADO &
BANANA PARFAIT

It is unusual to see avocado used in desserts, but this recipe is well worth a try.

Large ripe avocado 1
Bananas 2
Lime, grated rind and juice of 1
Unrefined brown sugar 2 oz (50 g)
Double cream ½ pt (300 ml)
Grated carob bar or fresh lime twists to decorate

Peel and remove stone from avocado. Peel bananas, and mash the fruit together roughly. Stir in the lime rind and juice and the sugar. Whip the double cream until stiff and fold in the fruit mixture. Transfer to individual glasses, decorate and serve at once.

Serves 6

BLACKBERRY & APPLE SNOW

Cooking apple 8 oz (225 g)
Blackberries 8 oz (225 g)
Unrefined brown sugar 2 oz (50 g)
Water 1 tbsp (15 ml)
Agar flakes 2 tbsp (30 ml) (see p. 4)
Egg whites 2
Whipped cream, blackberries and/or apple slices to decorate

Peel (if wished) core and roughly chop the apple. Place in a saucepan with the blackberries, half the sugar, water and agar flakes. Simmer gently for 10–15 minutes until tender. Leave to go cold. Whisk the egg whites until stiff, then whisk in the remaining sugar. Fold into the blackberry mixture and spoon into individual dishes. Top with cream, blackberries and apples.

Serves 4

PASKHA

Rich and delicious, this traditional Russian dish is
served at Easter. We have used Lebnie, a piquant
yoghourt cheese.

Sultanas 2 oz (50 g)
Brandy 1 tbsp (15 ml)
Unsalted butter 4 oz (100 g)
Unrefined brown sugar 2 oz (50 g)
Soured cream ¼ pt (150 ml)
Lebnie or cream cheese 5 oz (150 g)
Vanilla essence ½ tsp (2.5 ml)
Almonds, toasted and chopped 1 oz (25 g)
Carob bar, chopped 2 oz (50 g)
Fresh fruit or flaked almonds to decorate

Soak the sultanas in the brandy for several hours.
Cream the softened butter with the sugar until light and
fluffy. Add the soured cream, Lebnie and vanilla and
beat until smooth. Stir in the sultanas, chopped
almonds and chopped carob. Mix well. Spoon into a 1½
pt (900 ml) pudding basin, cover and refrigerate
overnight. When ready to serve, turn onto a plate and
decorate with fresh fruit or toasted flaked almonds.

Serves 6
***

LEMON MOUSSE

A light and refreshing dessert – ideal to round off an
elaborate dinner party.

Large lemon, grated rind & juice of 1
Unrefined brown sugar 4 oz (100 g)
Butter, diced 2 oz (50 g)
Free-range egg, beaten & strained 1
Egg white 1
Double cream ¼ pt (150 ml)
Fresh lemon slices and chopped pistachio nuts to decorate

Place lemon rind and juice in a basin with the sugar and
butter. Add the egg and place over a saucepan of
simmering water. Cook, stirring frequently for about
20–25 minutes until the mixture is thickened and coats
the back of a wooden spoon. Remove from the heat and
leave to go cold. Chill until required.

Whisk the egg white until stiff, whip the cream until
it just holds its shape. Fold the cream and then the egg
white into the lemon mixture. Transfer to individual
dishes and decorate with lemon slices and chopped
pistachio nuts. Serve at once.

Serves 4

HONEYCOMB MOUSSE

Try this unusually flavoured mousse based on an old
English recipe.

Milk 1 pt (600 ml)
Agar flakes 2 tbsp (30 ml) (see p. 4)
Bay leaves 2
Unrefined brown sugar 3 tbsp (45 ml)
Free-range eggs, separated 2

Heat the milk with the agar flakes, bay leaves and
sugar. Bring slowly to the boil then simmer for 2–3
minutes. Whisk in the egg yolks. Leave to cool, then
strain. Whisk the egg whites until stiff and fold into the
mixture. Transfer to a glass dish and leave in a cool
place to set.

Serves 4–6

PRUNE & ORANGE FOOL

Prunes 8 oz (225 g)
Orange, grated rind and juice of 1
Double cream ¼ pt (150 ml)
Egg whites 2
Orange slices to decorate

Just cover the prunes with water and leave to soak
overnight. Simmer for 15 minutes until tender, then
leave to go cold in the juice. Drain well.

Remove stones and purée in a liquidizer or food
processor. Stir in the orange rind and juice. Stiffly whip
the cream and egg whites and fold into the mixture.
Transfer to individual dishes and decorate with a twist
of orange.

Serves 4

YOGHOURT BRULEE

A 'creamy' mixture crusted with caramelized unrefined
sugar.

Egg yolks 4
Arrowroot 1 tbsp (15 ml)
Unrefined brown sugar 6 tbsp (90 ml)
Greek strained yoghourt 1 lb (450 g)
Green or black grapes to decorate

Beat the egg yolks, arrowroot and 2 tbsp (30 ml) sugar
until thick and pale. Stir in the yoghourt.

In a saucepan (preferably non-stick) cook the
yoghourt over the gentlest heat for 7–10 minutes,
stirring all the time, until thick enough to coat the back
of a wooden spoon.

Transfer the mixture to four individual ramekin
dishes. Level the surface and chill until required.

Just before serving, spread the surface of each dish
with 1 tbsp (15 ml) sugar, cook under a hot grill for 2–3
minutes until the sugar is melted. Chill until hardened,
then serve decorated with grapes.

Serves 4

HIGHLAND FLUMMERY

Easy to make and a lovely combination of texture and
flavour.

Butter 2 oz (50 g)
Almond flakes 2 oz (50 g)
Jumbo oats 1 oz (25 g)
Unrefined brown sugar 2 oz (50 g)
Double cream ½ pt (300 ml)
Fresh raspberries, roughly crushed 8 oz (225 g)
Raspberries and mint sprigs to decorate

Melt the butter and sauté the almonds and oats until
lightly golden. Stir in the sugar and cook, stirring over
medium heat until melted. Remove from the heat and
leave to go cold and brittle. Roughly crush the mixture.
Whip the cream and fold in the almond mixture and
raspberries. Divide between individual dishes, serve
decorated with raspberries and mint sprigs.

Serves 4

SPICED APPLE FOOL

An easy to make, light and simple dessert.

Cooking apples 8 oz (225 g)
Water 5 tbsp (75 ml)
Unrefined brown sugar 1½ oz (40 g)
Semolina ¾ oz (20 g)
Butter ½ oz (15 g)
Soured cream or
Greek strained yoghourt ¼ pt (150 ml)
Ground cinnamon 1 tsp (5 ml)
Slices of fresh apple to decorate

Wash and roughly chop the apples. Cook with the water and sugar to a soft pulp, about 10–15 minutes. Sieve the fruit and return to the pan with the semolina and butter. Bring slowly to the boil, stirring, then reduce heat, and simmer gently for about 5 minutes until thickened. Leave to go cold.

Stir in the soured cream and cinnamon and spoon into individual dishes.

Just before serving, decorate with slices of fresh apple.

Serves 4

STRAWBERRY SORBET

A delicious way to trap a glut of strawberries in the summer.

Fresh strawberries 1 lb (450 g)
Water ½ pt (300 ml)
Unrefined brown sugar 3 oz (75 g)
Lemon, juice of ½
Egg white 1

Wash and hull the strawberries and purée in a liquidizer or food processor. Combine the water, sugar and lemon juice in a small saucepan, stir over a low heat until the sugar has dissolved. Simmer for 3 minutes then allow to cool. Stir into the strawberry purée and freeze until almost frozen. Remove from the freezer and beat until smooth. Whisk the egg white until firm peaks form. Fold into the strawberry mixture. Freeze until firm.

Serves 4–6
***

GRAPEFRUIT SORBET

Large grapefruit 4
Water ½ pt (300 ml)
Unrefined brown sugar 3 oz (75 g)
Egg white 1

Grate the rind from two of the grapefruit and put into a saucepan with the water and sugar. Stir over a low heat until the sugar has dissolved. Bring to the boil, then simmer for three minutes. Cool. Stir in the juice of the four grapefruit and freeze until almost frozen. Remove from the freezer and beat until smooth. Whisk the egg white until firm peaks form, fold into the grapefruit mixture. Freeze until firm.

Serves 6
***

RASPBERRY YOGHOURT ICE CREAM

A wonderful way to use the flavour of fresh summer
raspberries.

Raspberries 1 lb (450 g)
Honey 2 tbsp (30 ml)
Natural yoghourt ¼ pt (150 ml)
Double cream, lightly whipped 8 fl oz (250 ml)

Pick over the raspberries then put them into the
liquidizer or food processor and blend until smooth.
Add the honey and yoghourt, blend again until
combined. Fold in the lightly whipped cream. Freeze
until almost frozen, then remove from the freezer and
beat until smooth. Freeze until firm.

Serves 4–6
***

PEACH & YOGHOURT ICE CREAM

Poached fresh peaches give this ice cream a wonderful
flavour.

Fresh peaches 2 lb (900 g)
Honey 2 tbsp (30 ml)
Natural yoghourt ¼ pt (150 ml)
Double cream, lightly whipped 8 fl oz (250 ml)

Place the peaches in boiling water and simmer gently
for 5 minutes. Transfer to cold water and cool in the
water. Peel, then purée them in a liquidizer or food
processor. Add the honey and yoghourt and blend
until combined. Fold in the lightly whipped cream.
Freeze until almost frozen, then remove from the
freezer and beat until smooth. Freeze until firm.

Serves 6–8
***

HAZELNUT PRALINE ICE CREAM

This ice cream does need care to make but gives a
beautifully creamy result and is well worth the effort!

PRALINE
Unrefined Demerara sugar 2 oz (50 g)
Water 3 tbsp (45 ml)
Hazelnuts, roasted 3 oz (75 g)

ICE CREAM
Unrefined Demerara sugar 3 oz (75 g)
Water 4 tbsp (60 ml)
Egg whites 4
Egg yolks 3
Decaffeinated coffee powder 1 tsp (5 ml)
mixed with water ½ tsp (2.5 ml)
Double cream, lightly whipped ¼ pt (150 ml)

First make the praline by dissolving the sugar in the
water over a very low heat. Bring to the boil and boil
without stirring until all the water has evaporated and a
light caramel has formed. Add the hazelnuts but do not
stir them in as this can make the caramel go sugary.
Pour onto a lightly oiled baking tray. When cold, blend
until fine in a liquidizer or food processor.
Alternatively, put the praline into a plastic bag and
crush it with a rolling pin.

Combine the sugar and water for the ice cream in a
small pan and stir over a low heat until the sugar has
dissolved. Bring to the boil and boil until most of the
water has evaporated and you are left with a thick
syrup. Do not let the sugar turn to caramel. Just before
the syrup is ready, whisk the egg whites until stiff, then
gradually add the syrup in a thin steady stream, beating
all the time. Beat until very thick and shiny. Whisk in
the yolks and the coffee mixture. Fold in the praline and
lightly whipped cream. Freeze until firm.

Serves 4–6
***

ICED CAROB MOUSSE

A tasty and useful sweet to have as a stand-by in the freezer. Take them out about 15 minutes before serving.

Carob bar 6 oz (175 g)
Butter 1 oz (25 g)
Free-range eggs, separated 3
Strong decaffeinated coffee 1 tbsp (15 ml)
Double cream ¼ pt (150 ml)
Chopped nuts to decorate

Melt the carob bar in a bowl over a saucepan of simmering water. Remove from the heat and stir in the butter and then the egg yolks and coffee. Leave to cool. Beat in 2 tbsp double cream, then stiffly whisk the egg whites and fold into the mixture. Transfer to four individual freezerproof dishes. Freeze until required.

Remove from the freezer, top with whipped cream and sprinkle with chopped nuts.

Serves 4
***

LINZERTORTE

Try the Cranks version of this delicious tart, the nut
pastry perfects it!

Wholemeal flour 3 oz (75 g)
Ground cinnamon ½ tsp (2.5 ml)
Unrefined brown sugar 3 oz (75 g)
Hazelnuts, ground 3 oz (75 g)
Butter 4 oz (100 g)
Egg yolks 2
Vanilla essence ½ tsp (2.5 ml)
Lemon, grated rind of ½
Unrefined sugar black cherry jam 8 oz (225 g)

Mix the flour, cinnamon, sugar and hazelnuts together.
Rub in the butter, then add the egg yolks, vanilla
essence and lemon rind and work to a firm dough.
Press three-quarters of the dough evenly over the base
and sides of an 8 in (20 cm) French fluted flan tin. Wrap
the reserved pastry and chill it and the pastry case for 30
minutes.

Roll out the reserved pastry and cut into strips to fit
across the flan tin.

Spread jam over the base of the pastry case and
arrange the pastry strips in a lattice effect on the top.
Neaten the edges.

Bake at 375°F/190°C/gas mark 5 for 35–40 minutes.
Serve warm or cold.

Serves 6–8
***

ORANGE TART

This tangy citrus filling complements the texture of our rich pastry.

Rich wholemeal shortcrust pastry 1 quantity (see p. 9)
Medium-sized oranges 3
Butter, melted 2 oz (50 g)
Free-range eggs 3
Wholemeal sponge cake crumbs 1 oz (25 g) (see p. 10)
Unrefined brown sugar 3 oz (75 g)
Lemon juice 1 tbsp (15 ml)

Roll out the pastry on a lightly floured surface and use to line an 8 in (20 cm) French fluted flan tin. Bake blind at 375°F/190°C/gas mark 5 for 20 minutes.

Grate the rind from the oranges and squeeze the juice from two. Combine this with the remaining ingredients and beat well. Pour into the half-baked pastry case and bake for a further 25 minutes until set. Leave to go cold.

Carefully peel the remaining orange removing all the white pith. Cut in to thin slices, then halve each one. Arrange the halved orange slices around the edge of the tart.

Serves 6–8
***

MAPLE SYRUP TART

Maple syrup gives such a special flavour to this tart.

Wholemeal pastry made
using wholemeal flour 4 oz (100 g) (see chart p. 7)
Maple syrup 6 fl oz (175 ml)
Ground almonds 2 oz (50 g)
Fresh wholemeal breadcrumbs 2 oz (50 g)
Double cream 4 tbsp (60ml)
Free-range egg 1
Lemon, grated rind of ½

Roll out the pastry and use to line an 8 in (20 cm) French fluted flan tin. Beat together all the remaining ingredients and pour into the pastry case.

Bake at 375°F/190°C/gas mark 5 for about 35 minutes until just set and golden brown. Serve warm or cold.

Serves 6–8
***

MARZIPAN PLUM TART

A rich moist almond mixture combined with fresh
plums makes an ideal filling for this tart.

Rich wholemeal shortcrust pastry 1 quantity (see p. 9)
Butter 3 oz (75 g)
Unrefined brown sugar 3 oz (75 g)
Free-range egg, beaten 1
Ground almonds 3 oz (75 g)
Almonds, chopped 1 oz (25 g)
Wholemeal flour 2 tbsp (30 ml)
Fresh plums, stoned and chopped 8 oz (225 g)

Roll out the pastry and use to line a deep-sided 8 in
(20 cm) French fluted flan tin.

Cream the butter and sugar until pale and fluffy. Beat
in the egg, then fold in the remaining ingredients until
evenly mixed. Transfer to flan case and level the
surface.

Bake at 375°F/190°C/gas mark 5 for 50 minutes to
1 hour until golden brown and firm to the touch. Serve
warm or cold.

Serves 6–8
***

BLACKCURRANT & APPLE PLATE PIE

Rich wholemeal shortcrust pastry double quantity (see p. 9)
Cooking apples, peeled, cored & sliced 1½ lb (675 g)
Blackcurrants or blueberries 8 oz (225 g)
Unrefined brown sugar 2 oz (50 g)

On a lightly floured surface roll out half the pastry and use to line 10–11 in (25–28 cm) ovenproof pie plate. Arrange half the apple slices on the pastry, top with the blackcurrants and sprinkle with the sugar. Top with remaining apple slices. Roll out remaining pastry to a circle large enough to fit over the pie. Damp the edges of the pie and cover with the pastry. Seal the edges well then trim and neaten. Make a slit in the top of the pastry then bake the pie at 400°F/200°C/gas mark 6 for 25 minutes. Reduce heat to 350°F/180°C/gas mark 4 and cook for a further 25–30 minutes until golden. Serve warm or cold with cream or ice cream.

Serves 8

AVOCADO & LIME CHIFFON PIE

The smoothness of the avocado complements the tangy flavour of lime in this delicious and unusual pie. It keeps well and holds its colour.

Rich wholemeal shortcrust pastry 1 quantity (see p. 9)
Arrowroot 3 tbsp (45 ml)
Water or milk ¼ pt (150 ml)
Unrefined brown sugar 6 tbsp (90 ml)
Limes, grated rind & juice of 3
Egg yolks 4
Agar flakes 1 tbsp (15 ml) (see p. 4)
Water 4 tbsp (60 ml)
Ripe avocado 1
Egg whites 2
Whipped cream and lime slices to decorate

Roll out the pastry and use to line an 8 in (20 cm) deep-sided French fluted flan tin.

Bake blind at 400°F/200°C/gas mark 6 for 25–30 minutes until completely baked. Leave to go cold. Mix the arrowroot with the milk and half the sugar.

Stir in the lime rind and juice and the egg yolks and cook over gentle heat, stirring until thickened.

Dissolve the agar flakes in the measured water over gentle heat, and bring to the boil.

Peel and roughly mash the avocado. Combine the lime custard, agar and avocado together and purée in a liquidizer or food processor.

Whisk the egg whites until stiff, then whisk in remaining sugar. Fold into avocado mixture. Transfer to baked pastry case and chill until set. Decorate with whipped cream and lime slices.

Serves 6–8

Brown Sugar Meringues with Bramble Sauce, page 21
Autumn Pudding, page 23
Poached Pears in White Wine, page 20

Crusted Apple Dumplings, page 46
Plymouth Peak Pudding with Custard Sauce, page 60
Fruit Buckwheat Roll ups, page 49

Avocado & Lime Chiffon Pie, page 40
Continental Apple Flan, page 45
Banana & Coconut Cream Pie, page 41

Florentine Pie, page 42
Linzertorte, page 35
Marzipan Plum Tart, page 37

Lemon Mousse, page 26
Wholemeal Sponge Fingers, page 10
Avocado & Banana Parfait, page 24
Yoghourt Brulée, page 28

Grapefruit Sorbet, page 31
Yellow Fruit Salad, page 18
Chestnut, Apricot & Orange Compote
  with Cranks Flapjacks, page 19

Carrot Cake Pudding with Cinnamon Cream, page 69
Carob Truffle Gateau, page 75
Walnut Gateau, page 74

Sherried Syllabub Trifle, page 71
Macaroons, page 9
Pavlova Nests, page 66
Orange & Strawberry Terrine, page 16

BANANA & COCONUT CREAM PIE

Although coconut milk powder gives a delicate flavour to this delicious pie, skimmed milk powder may be substituted.

Rich wholemeal shortcrust pastry 1 quantity (see p. 9)
Natural yoghourt ¼ pt (150 ml)
Coconut milk powder 2 oz (50 g)
Curd cheese 6 oz (175 g)
Cream cheese 6 oz (175 g)
Honey 5 tbsp (75 ml)
Bananas 2

Roll out the pastry on a lightly floured surface and use to line an 8 in (20 cm) deep-sided French fluted flan tin. Bake blind at 400°F/200°C/gas mark 6 for 20 minutes. Place the yoghourt, coconut milk powder cheese and 3 tablespoons (45 ml) honey in a liquidizer or food processor and blend until smooth. Transfer to the pastry case, level the surface and bake for 20 minutes until lightly set. Leave to go cold.

Just before serving, thinly slice the bananas and arrange on top of the pie. Drizzle with reserved honey and serve at once.

Note: Other fruits may be substituted for the banana, for example fresh nectarines or peaches.

Serves 6–8

FLORENTINE PIE

Try different combinations of nuts to vary the flavour of this pie.

Wholemeal pastry made with flour 5 oz (150 g)
(see chart, p. 7)

Butter 4 oz (100 g)
Unrefined brown sugar 4 oz (100 g)
Free-range eggs, beaten 3
Honey 4 tbsp (60 ml)
Lemon, juice of ½
Ground cinnamon ½ tsp (2.5 ml)
Mixed nuts, chopped 4 oz (100 g)

Roll out pastry and use to line an 8 in (20 cm) deep-sided French fluted flan tin. Cream the butter and sugar until pale and fluffy. Beat in the eggs, then stir in the remaining ingredients. Pour into the flan case and bake at 375°F/190°C/gas mark 5 for about 45 minutes until just set. Leave to cool in the tin. Serve just warm or cold.

Serves 6–8
***

PUMPKIN PIE

The Cranks version of an American favourite.

Rich wholemeal shortcrust pastry 1 quantity (see p. 9)
Pumpkin purée 8 oz (225 g)
Free-range eggs 2
Unrefined brown sugar 2 oz (50 g)
Double cream 4 fl oz (100 ml)
Ground cinnamon ½ tsp (2.5 ml)
Ground ginger ½ tsp (2.5 ml)
Ground cloves ¼ tsp (1.25 ml)
Ground nutmeg ¼ tsp (1.25 ml)
Whipped cream and pumpkin seeds or pecan halves to decorate

Roll out the pastry on a lightly floured surface and use to line an 8 in (20 cm) deep-sided French fluted flan tin. Bake blind at 375°F/190°C/gas mark 5 for 20 minutes.

Mix all the ingredients for the filling in a liquidizer or food processor. Pour into the par-baked pastry case and cook for a further 35 minutes until set. Leave to go cold. If wished, decorate with swirls of whipped cream and pumpkin seeds or pecan halves.

Serves 6–8
***

Note: To make pumpkin purée, bake wedges of pumpkin on a baking sheet at 350°F/180°C/gas mark 4 for about 45 minutes until tender, discard seeds and skin. Purée flesh in a liquidizer or food processor.

COFFEE FUDGE PIE

This pie is so popular in our shops and restaurants that our bakery finds it difficult to keep up with the demand. We use a sugar free jam which is now widely available.

Wholemeal pastry made with wholemeal flour 7 oz (200 g)
(see chart, p. 7)

Butter 5 oz (150 g)
Unrefined brown sugar 5 oz (150 g)
Free-range eggs, beaten 3
Decaffeinated instant coffee powder 2 tbsp (30 ml)
Self-raising wholemeal flour 6 oz (175 g)
Walnuts, chopped 4 oz (100 g)
Milk 1 tbsp (15 ml)
Apricot jam 3 oz (75 g)
Soured cream ¼ pt (150 ml)

Roll out the pastry and use to line a 10 in (25 cm) French fluted flan tin. Cream the butter and sugar until pale and fluffy. Beat in the eggs, then fold in the decaffeinated coffee powder, flour and 3 oz (75 g) walnuts. Stir in the milk. Spread the base of the pastry with apricot jam, then spread the coffee mixture evenly on top.

Bake at 375°F/190°C/gas mark 5 for about 35 minutes until just set. Carefully spread the soured cream over the surface of the pie and sprinkle with reserved nuts. Return to the oven for 5 minutes. Serve warm or cold.

Serves 10
(without topping)
***

CONTINENTAL APPLE FLAN

A Cranks variation of this classic dessert.

Rich wholemeal shortcrust pastry 1 quantity (see p. 9)
Cooking apples 1½ lb (675 g)
Water 1 tbsp (15 ml)
Unrefined brown sugar 3 oz (75 g)
Ground cinnamon 1 tsp (5 ml)
Sultanas 2 oz (50 g)
Ground almonds 2 oz (50 g)
Eating apple 1
Butter, melted 1 tbsp (15 ml)
Unrefined demerara sugar 1 tbsp (15 ml)

Roll out the pastry on a lightly floured surface and use to line an 8 in (20 cm) deep-sided French fluted flan tin. Bake blind at 375°F/190°C/gas mark 5 for about 30 minutes until completely cooked and crisp. Leave to go cold.

Peel, core and chop the apples and cook with the water, sugar, cinnamon and sultanas until tender and pulpy (about 10–15 minutes). Leave to go cold, then stir in the ground almonds and use to fill the flan case. Quarter, core and very thinly slice the apple. Arrange the slices attractively over the apple purée. Brush with melted butter and sprinkle with demerara sugar. Place under a medium hot grill for about 5 minutes to glaze the apples. Leave to go cold.

Serves 6–8
***

CRUSTED APPLE DUMPLINGS

Vary the flavour of these apple dumplings by changing
the stuffing.

Small cooking apples 4
Cranks mincemeat 4 tbsp (60 ml) (see p. 14)
Wholemeal pastry made with flour 10 oz (300 g) (see p. 7)
Egg yolk 1
Soured cream 1 tbsp (15 ml)

Peel and core the apples. Fill the centres with the
mincemeat. Roll out the pastry quite thinly and cut into
four pieces large enough to completely encase the
apples. Place an apple in the centre of each piece of
pastry. Brush the edges with combined beaten egg yolk
and soured cream. Fold the corners of pastry up and
over the apple to completely cover it. Press the edges
together firmly to give a neat shape. Brush with the egg
mixture and decorate with pastry trimmings. Bake in
the oven at 400°F/200°C/gas mark 6 for 25–30 minutes or
until golden. Serve with custard sauce (see p. 13).

Serves 4
***

TOFU "CHEESE CAKE"

A sugar free special dessert served regularly in Cranks restaurants. Suitable for those on a dairy-free diet.

BASE
Wholemeal flour 4 oz (100 g)
Jumbo oats 4 oz (100 g)
Margarine, melted 3 oz (75 g)
Malt extract 1 oz (25 g)
Ground cinnamon 1 tsp (5 ml)

FILLING
Dates, chopped 6 oz (175 g)
Water 8 fl oz (225 ml)
Apple concentrate 4 fl oz (100 ml) (see p. 4)
Tahini 1 tsp (5 ml) (see p. 6)
Lemon, grated rind & juice of 1
Ground mixed spice ½ tsp (2.5 ml)
Agar flakes 2 tsp (10ml) (see p. 4)
Tofu 1 lb (450 g) (see p. 6)
Fresh fruit of your choice to decorate

Combine all the ingredients for the base and press onto the base of an 8 in (20 cm) spring release tin. Chill. Cook the dates in the water until soft – about 10 minutes. Leave to go cold.

Place all the ingredients for the filling in a liquidizer or food processor, and work to a smooth mixture. Pour over the base and bake at 350°F/180°C/gas mark 4 for about 45 minutes until set and golden. Leave to go cold, then unmould. Decorate with the prepared fruit of your choice, such as orange segments and kiwi slices.

Serves 8 –10

CONTINENTAL CHEESECAKE

BASE
Digestive biscuit crumbs 8 oz (225 g)
Butter or margarine 3 oz (75 g)

TOPPING
Butter or margarine 4 oz (100 g)
Vanilla essence ½ tsp (2.5 ml)
Lemon, grated rind of ½
Unrefined brown sugar 3 oz (75 g)
Free-range eggs 3
Cottage cheese, sieved 1 lb (450 g)
Soured cream ¼ pt (150 ml)
Double cream, whipped 8 fl oz (250 ml)
Carob bar 2 oz (50 g)

Base

Combine the biscuit crumbs and melted butter, then press evenly over the base of a 7 in × 11 in (18 cm × 28 cm) cake tin which has been lined with foil. Refrigerate while preparing the filling.

Filling

Beat the butter, vanilla, lemon rind and sugar until light and fluffy. Add the eggs, one at a time, beating well after each addition. Add the sieved cottage cheese and soured cream, beat until smooth. Spread over the base, bake in the oven at 325°F/170°C/gas mark 3 for 40–50 minutes until firm to the touch. Cool, then refrigerate until ready to serve. Reserve 1 tbsp (15 ml) cream then top the cheesecake with the remaining whipped cream. Put the chopped carob bar and reserved cream into a small basin. Rest over a pan of simmering water and stir until the carob has melted. Spoon the carob mixture into the corner of a small greaseproof paper piping bag, snip the corner, then drizzle the carob over the top of the cream.

Serves 8
***

FRUIT BUCKWHEAT ROLL UPS

A chunky fruit filling encased in a buckwheat pancake.

Dried apricots, soaked overnight 4 oz (100 g)
Prepared fresh pineapple 8 oz (225 g)
Sultanas 2 oz (50 g)
Fruit juice, e.g. orange
or pineapple ½ pt (300 ml)
Arrowroot 2 tsp (10 ml)
Buckwheat pancakes 8 (see p. 12)
Unrefined brown sugar 1 tbsp (15 ml)

Drain and roughly chop the apricots, and chop the
pineapple. Add the sultanas. Mix the fruit juice and
arrowroot together and cook, stirring until thickened.
Stir in the fruit. Divide the filling between the prepared
pancakes and roll up. Arrange in a single layer in an
ovenproof dish. Sprinkle with the sugar and heat gently
under the grill until the surface is bubbling.

Serves 4
***

BAKED DUSKY CUSTARD

Unrefined brown sugar 5 tbsp (75 ml)
Egg yolks 6
Milk, warmed ¾ pt (450 ml)

Place 3 tbsp (45 ml) sugar in a saucepan and stir over
moderate heat until the sugar melts. Remove from the
heat and carefully add 1 tbsp (15 ml) water. Return the
pan to the heat and stir to a thick syrup. Immediately
pour it into a 1½ pt (900 ml) souffle dish. Whisk the egg
yolks with the remaining sugar until thick and pale. Stir
in the milk and strain into the souffle dish. Place in a
roasting pan with boiling water to come half way up the
sides of the dish and bake at 300°F/150°C/gas mark 2 for
1½ hours until set. Leave to go cold then unmould on to
a flat plate. Serve with fresh fruit, if wished.

Serves 4

SWEET CHEESE PARCELS

These exciting little parcels can be prepared in advance
ready to pop under the grill when needed – they are
delicious!

Cream cheese 8 oz (225 g)
Eating apple, cored and finely chopped 1
Raisins 2 oz (50 g)
Ground cinnamon 1 tsp (5 ml)
Unrefined brown sugar 3 tbsp (45 ml)
Lemon, grated rind and juice of 1
Buckwheat pancakes 1 quantity (see p. 12)
Butter, melted 1 oz (25 g)

Mix together the cream cheese, apple, raisins,
cinnamon, two tablespoons of sugar and the lemon
rind and juice. Divide the mixture between the
pancakes and fold up to completely encase the filling.
Arrange in a heatproof serving dish in a single layer.
Brush with melted butter and sprinkle with remaining
sugar. Heat gently under a preheated grill until just
warm. Serve at once.

Serves 4
***

PRUNE & ALMOND STIRABOUT

Large prunes, soaked overnight 24
Whole almonds 24
Wholemeal flour 2 oz (50 g)
Salt, a pinch
Free-range eggs, beaten 3
Unrefined brown sugar 1 oz (25 g)
Butter 1 oz (25 g)
Milk ¾ pt (450 ml)
Dark rum, optional 3 tbsp (45 ml)

Just cover the prunes with water and simmer for 10–15 minutes until tender. Drain, leave to go cold then remove the stones and replace with whole almonds. Arrange in a greased 10 × 12 in (25 × 30 cm) baking dish. Place flour, salt, eggs and sugar in a bowl. Bring the milk and butter to the boil and slowly whisk into the flour until evenly mixed. Stir in the rum.

Pour the batter over the prunes and bake at 400°F/ 200°C/gas mark 6 for about 40 minutes until set and golden. Serve warm.

Serves 6

HOT APRICOT SOUFFLE

This souffle will not wait for the guests – so make sure they're ready!

Dried apricots 6 oz (175 g)
Water ½ pt (300 ml)
Butter 1½ oz (40 g)
Wholemeal flour 4 tbsp (60 ml)
Milk ¼ pt (150 ml)
Unrefined brown sugar 2 oz (50 g)
Free-range eggs, separated 4

Soak the apricots in the measured water for up to 24 hours. Purée with their liquid. Grease a 3 pt (1.8 l) souffle dish. Melt the butter and stir in the flour. Cook for 1 minute, then stir in the milk and bring slowly to the boil. Reduce heat, stir in the sugar and egg yolks and beat well. Remove from the heat and stir in the apricot purée. Stiffly whisk the egg whites and fold in. Transfer to the prepared souffle dish and bake at 350°F/ 180°C/gas mark 4 for about 55 minutes until risen and just set when lightly shaken. Serve at once.

Serves 6

GOOSEBERRY MUESLI CRUMBLE

Gooseberries 1 lb (450 g)
Unrefined brown sugar 4 oz (100 g)
Wholemeal flour 3 oz (75 g)
Muesli 3 oz (75 g)
Butter, melted 2 oz (50 g)

Top and tail the gooseberries and simmer with 1 oz (25 g) sugar and 1 tbsp (15 ml) of water until just tender. Cool and transfer to a 1½ pt (900 ml) pie dish.

Mix the remaining ingredients together and spoon over the fruit, pressing down gently. Bake at 375°F/ 190°C/gas mark 5 for about 30 minutes.

Serves 4
***

BANANA & CASHEW NUT SLICE

A very popular sugar and dairy-free dessert served regularly on Cranks buffet counter.

Soya oil 4 fl oz (100 ml)
Bananas, peeled and mashed 1 lb (450 g)
Vanilla essence 1 tsp (5 ml)
Cashew nut pieces 3 oz (75 g)
Desiccated coconut 3 oz (75 g)
Rolled oats 3 oz (75 g)
Ground cinnamon 2 tsp (10 ml)
Ground cardamom ½ tsp (2.5 ml)

Grease and base line a 9 inch (23 cm) sandwich tin. Whisk oil and banana until very smooth. Fold in all other ingredients and mix well. Turn into prepared tin. Level the surface. Bake at 400°F/200°C/gas mark 6 for 20–25 minutes until firm to the touch. Cool in tin then cut into wedges.

Serves 8

CHERRY FLAPJACK CRUMBLE

In this recipe we have used cherries but any fresh soft
fruit may be substituted.

Fresh cherries, pitted 1 lb (450 g)
Wholemeal flour 2 oz (50 g)
Desiccated coconut 2 oz (50 g)
Porridge oats 2 oz (50 g)
Unrefined brown sugar 1 oz (25 g)
Butter or margarine, melted 1½ oz (40 g)
Clear honey 2 tbsp (30 ml)

Place the cherries in a 1½ pt (900 ml) pie dish. Mix
together the flour, coconut, porridge oats and sugar.
Stir in the butter or margarine and honey and mix well
until evenly coated. Sprinkle over the fruit, starting at
the outside edge and working towards the centre,
pressing down gently.

Bake at 375°F/190°C/gas mark 5 for 25–30 minutes
until golden.

Serves 4
***

CRANKS BREAD & BUTTER PUDDING

We use Cranks wholemeal bread in this age-old recipe –
try it!

Thinly sliced wholemeal bread 4 oz (100 g)
Butter 1 oz (25 g)
Sultanas 2 oz (50 g)
Milk 1 pt (600 ml)
Free-range eggs 3
Unrefined brown sugar 2 oz (50 g)
Freshly grated nutmeg, to sprinkle

Butter the slices of bread and arrange in a 1½ pt (900 ml)
oven-proof dish. Sprinkle the sultanas over the top.
Heat the milk to just below boiling. Whisk the eggs and
sugar until pale, then stir in the milk. Strain the mixture
over the bread and leave to soak for 15 minutes.
Sprinkle with freshly grated nutmeg.

Place the dish in a roasting tin and pour in sufficient
boiling water to come half way up the sides of the dish.
Bake at 325°F/170°C/gas mark 3 for 30–45 minutes until
lightly set. Serve warm.

Variation
For a creamier custard, replace half the milk with
double cream.

Serves 4

NUTTY PLUM CRUMBLE

A really wholesome treat!

Fresh plums, halved and stoned 1 lb (450 g)
Unrefined brown sugar 2 oz (50 g)
Wholemeal flour 2 oz (50 g)
Jumbo oats 2 oz (50 g)
Desiccated coconut 2 oz (50 g)
Sunflower seeds 1 oz (25 g)
Walnuts, chopped 2 oz (50 g)
Butter or margarine 2 oz (50 g)
Malt extract 2 tbsp (30 ml)

Cook the plums and sugar with 1 tbsp (15 ml) water for
about 10 minutes until just tender. Place in a 1½ pt (900
ml) pie dish. Mix together all the dry ingredients. Warm
the butter or margarine and malt extract together and
stir into the mixture, until evenly combined. Sprinkle
the crumble mixture over the plums, pressing down
gently.

Bake at 375°F/190°C/gas mark 5 for 30 minutes until
golden brown. Serve with warm custard sauce (see
p. 13) or fresh cream.

Serves 4
***

STEAMED CAROB CHIP PUDDING

An easy-to-make traditional steamed sponge pudding.

Butter or margarine 3 oz (75 g)
Honey 4 oz (100 g)
Free-range eggs 2
Self-raising wholemeal flour 6 oz (175 g)
Carob bar, broken into chips 2 oz (50 g)
Raisins 3 oz (75 g)
Walnuts, chopped 3 oz (75 g)
Milk 1 tbsp (15 ml)

Grease a 2 pt (1.2 l) pudding basin. Cream the butter and honey until pale, beat in the eggs, then fold in the remaining ingredients. Transfer the mixture to the prepared basin. Level the surface, then make a slight dip in the centre. Cut a large circle of kitchen foil or greaseproof paper and lightly grease. Make a pleat in the centre and carefully cover the pudding, sealing the edges well. Either steam or cook the pudding in a large saucepan of simmering water for about 1¾ hours until risen and firm to the touch. Unmould and serve with custard sauce. (see p. 13)

Serves 4–6
***

YANKIE NOODLE PUDDING

The name suggests the origin of this rich milk pudding!

Wholemeal pasta noodles 5 oz (150 g)
Soured cream ¼ pt (150 ml)
Cream cheese 4 oz (100 g)
Unrefined brown sugar 3 oz (75 g)
Free-range eggs, separated 2
Milk 8 fl oz (250 ml)
Ground cinnamon 1 tsp (5 ml)
Cream cheese 4 oz (100 g)

Cook the pasta in boiling water for 10 minutes. Drain.
Beat together the soured cream, cream cheese, 2 oz
(50 g) sugar and egg yolks. Stir in the milk. Whisk the
egg whites until stiff and fold through the mixture.
Place the noodles in a greased 10 × 8 in (25 × 20 cm)
shallow baking dish. Pour the mixture over. Mix
remaining sugar with the cinnamon and sprinkle on
top. Bake at 400°F/200°C/gas mark 6 for about 1 hour
until just set. Leave to stand for 5 minutes before
serving.

Serves 6

STICKY FIG PUDDING

Serve this sticky moist pudding with cream or custard sauce. (see p. 13)

(see p. 13)

Dried figs 4 oz (100 g)
Unrefined brown sugar 4 oz (100 g)
Vegetable oil 4 fl oz (100 ml)
Free-range eggs 2
Wholemeal flour 5 oz (150 g)
Bicarbonate of soda ½ tsp (2.5 ml)
Ground cinnamon 1 tsp (5 ml)
Ground nutmeg ½ tsp (2.5 ml)
Ground mixed spice ½ tsp (2.5 ml)
Buttermilk or natural yoghourt 4 fl oz (100 ml)

TOPPING
Unrefined brown sugar 2 oz (50 g)
Buttermilk or natural yoghourt 3 tbsp (45 ml)
Maple syrup or honey 1 tbsp (15 ml)

Grease a 1¾ pt (1 l) pie dish. Just cover the figs with water, bring to the boil, then simmer for 5–7 minutes until soft. Drain well and roughly chop. In a bowl whisk together the sugar, oil and eggs until smooth. Stir in the flour, bicarbonate of soda and spices. Beat well, then fold in the figs and buttermilk or yoghourt.

Transfer the mixture to the prepared dish and bake at 350°F/180°C/gas mark 4 for about 45 minutes until risen and firm to the touch.

Warm the ingredients for the topping in a saucepan. Prick the pudding with a skewer and pour the syrup over. Leave until just soaked in, then serve.

Serves 6
***

PLYMOUTH PEAK PUDDING

Named after Plymouth, Massachusetts, USA, famous
for its cranberries. The traditional Christmas
ingredients makes it a good alternative to the British
Christmas pudding.

Cranberries 6 oz (175 g)
Unrefined sugar mincemeat 6 oz (175 g) (see p. 14)
Flaked or chopped almonds 1 oz (25 g)
Butter or margarine 4 oz (100 g)
Unrefined brown sugar 4 oz (100 g)
Free-range eggs, beaten 2
Self-raising wholemeal flour 4 oz (100g)
Ground almonds 2 oz (50 g)

Place the cranberries in a saucepan with 1 tbsp (15 ml)
water. Simmer gently until they just start to pop.
Remove from the heat, stir in the mincemeat and
almonds. Place in the bottom of a greased 2½ pt (1.5 l)
pudding basin. Cream the butter or margarine and
sugar until pale and fluffy. Beat in the eggs a little at a
time, then fold in the flour and ground almonds. Spoon
this mixture over the cranberries, spreading it evenly.
Cover with a large round of buttered greaseproof paper
or foil and steam for 1¾–2 hours until risen and firm to
the touch. Unmould on to a serving plate and serve
with custard sauce (see p. 13) or cream.

Serves 6
***

RHUBARB & GINGER SPONGE PUDDING

A lovely fruit layer under a baked sponge crust.

Rhubarb 1½ lb (675 g)
Unrefined brown sugar 2 oz (50 g)
Unrefined sugar crystallized ginger, chopped 1½ oz (40 g)

SPONGE
Butter or margarine 4 oz (100 g)
Unrefined brown sugar 4 oz (100 g)
Free-range eggs, beaten 2
Self-raising wholemeal flour 4 oz (100 g)
Ground ginger 1 tsp (5 ml)

Trim the rhubarb and cut into 1 in (2.5 cm) lengths. Place in a saucepan with the sugar and cook over gentle heat for 10–15 minutes until just tender. Stir in chopped ginger. Transfer to a 2 pt (1.2 l) capacity ovenproof dish.

Cream the butter and sugar until pale and fluffy. Beat in the eggs a little at a time, then fold in the flour and ginger. Cover the rhubarb with the sponge mixture and bake at 350°F/180°C/gas mark 4 for about 40 minutes until the sponge is risen and firm to the touch. Serve with custard sauce (see p. 13) or cream.

Serves 4–6
***

SURPRISE LEMON PUDDING

The 'surprise' is the layer of lemon sauce underneath the sponge.

Butter 2 oz (50 g)
Unrefined brown sugar 4 oz (100 g)
Free-range eggs, separated 2
Self-raising wholemeal flour 2 oz (50 g)
Lemon, grated rind & juice of 1
Milk ½ pt (300 ml)

Cream the butter and sugar until pale and fluffy. Beat in the egg yolks, then fold in the flour. Stir in the lemon rind and juice and milk a little at a time. Stiffly whisk the egg whites and fold into the mixture. Transfer to a 1¾ pt (1 l) ovenproof serving dish. Place the dish in a roasting tin and pour boiling water to come at least halfway up the side of the dish. Bake at 400°F/200°C/gas mark 6 for about 35 minutes until risen and firm to the touch. Serve at once.

Serves 4

BROWN RICE PUDDING WITH SULTANAS

To achieve the best results for this delicious old-fashioned recipe the whole rice grains should be soaked overnight.

Short grain brown rice 4 oz (100 g)
Milk 1 pt (600 ml)
Unrefined brown sugar 2 tbsp (30 ml)
Butter or margarine 1 oz (25 g)
Strips of lemon rind 2
Sultanas 2 oz (50 g)

Wash the rice well, then cover with ½ pt (300 ml) water and leave to soak for at least 1 hour, or longer if possible. Add remaining ingredients, except the sultanas and bring slowly to the boil. Reduce heat, cover and simmer for about 1½ hours until tender, stirring occasionally. Stir in sultanas, and add extra milk, if wished.

Variation
Alternatively, bake the rice pudding at 300°F/150°C/gas mark 2 for 1½–2 hours. Add sultanas just before serving.

Serves 4

MEDITERRANEAN MERINGUE

Crisp yet chewy meringue discs sandwiched together with fresh cream – an elaborate dinner party dessert.

Egg whites 4
Unrefined brown sugar 8 oz (225 g)
Stoned dates, chopped 3 oz (75 g)
Walnuts, chopped 3 oz (75 g)
Orange, grated rind of 1
Double cream, whipped ½–¾ pt (300–450 ml)
Orange slices and walnut halves to decorate

Cut out two 8 in (20 cm) circles of non-stick paper and place on baking sheets. Whisk the egg whites until stiff, then whisk in the sugar a spoonful at a time until very thick. Fold in the dates, walnuts and grated orange rind. Divide the mixture between the two circles, spreading it evenly. Bake at 140°C/275°F/gas mark 1 for 2 hours. Leave to go cold, then remove lining paper and sandwich together with whipped cream.

Decorate the top with more whipped cream, if wished, and orange slices and walnut halves.

Serves 8

MINCEMEAT MERINGUE SHORTBREAD

This recipe combines shortbread and meringue, two of the most popular sweet bakes of all time. Serve it at Christmas as an alternative to mince pies.

BASE
Wholemeal flour 5 oz (150 g)
Brown rice flour 1 oz (25 g)
Butter 4 oz (100 g)
Unrefined brown sugar 2 oz (50 g)

TOPPING
Unrefined sugar mincemeat 8 oz (225 g) (see p. 14)
Egg whites 2
Unrefined brown sugar 2 oz (50 g)
Arrowroot 1 tsp (5 ml)
Ground almonds 2 oz (50 g)

Mix the flours together, then rub in the butter and add the sugar. Work together with your fingertips to form a firm dough. Press evenly over the base of a 11 × 7 in (28 × 18 cm) tin and bake at 150°C/300°F/gas mark 2 for 40 minutes. Cool slightly and spread with mincemeat. Whisk the egg whites until stiff, then whisk in the sugar a tablespoonful at a time. Fold in the arrowroot and ground almonds. Spread evenly over the mincemeat and return to the oven for 20 minutes until golden.

Serve warm or cold.

Serves 8
***

PAVLOVA NESTS

Individual pavlova nests are so much easier to serve than the usual full-sized one which crumbles easily!

Egg whites 4
Unrefined brown sugar, sifted 8 oz (225 g)
Cider vinegar 2 tsp (10 ml)
Arrowroot 1 tsp (5 ml)
Double cream, whipped ½ pt (300 ml)
Prepared fresh fruit of your choice,
such as mango, pineapple 12 oz–1 lb (350 g–450 g)

Draw six 4 in (10 cm) circles on a large sheet of non-stick paper placed on a baking tray. Whisk the egg whites until just stiff, then whisk in the sugar a spoonful at a time until very thick. Whisk in the vinegar and arrowroot. Divide the mixture between the six circles and shape into 'nests'. Bake at 120°C/250°F/gas mark ½ for 1 hour. Leave to go cold on the tray. Just before serving fill with fresh cream and prepared fruit.

Serves 6

GOOSEBERRY CHARLOTTE

For a special occasion tie a ribbon around the sponge
fingers.

Gooseberries, topped and tailed 1 lb (450 g)
Unrefined brown sugar 3 oz (75 g)
Water 6 tbsp (90 ml)
Agar flakes 4 tbsp (60 ml) (see p. 4)
Egg yolks 2
Milk ½ pt (300 ml)
Double cream ½ pt (300 ml)
Wholemeal sponge fingers (see p. 10), halved crossways 8–10
Poached gooseberries to decorate

Cook the gooseberries with 2 oz (50 g) sugar and the
water until tender. Purée and sieve to remove the pips.
Return to a clean saucepan with the agar flakes. Bring to
the boil, reduce heat and simmer gently for about 3
minutes, stirring until the agar is dissolved. Cool.

Beat the egg yolks with the remaining sugar. Warm
the milk and pour on to the eggs. Strain back into the
pan and then cook over very gentle heat, stirring until
the custard coats the back of a wooden spoon. Stir into
the gooseberry purée. Cool. Whip half the cream and
fold into the gooseberry mixture. Pour into a 1½ pt
(900 ml) souffle dish and chill until set. Unmould onto a
flat plate. Whip the cream and spread the sides thinly
with a little of the cream. Press sponge fingers evenly
onto the sides. Pipe the remaining cream onto the top of
the charlotte and decorate with poached gooseberries, if
wished.

Serves 6

CRANKS CHRISTMAS PUDDING

Cranks traditional Christmas Pudding made to order in our bakeries.

Wholemeal breadcrumbs 6oz (175 g)
Wholemeal flour 3 oz (75 g)
Currants 8 oz (225 g)
Raisins 8 oz (225 g)
Sultanas 8 oz (225 g)
Almonds, chopped 1 oz (25 g)
Unrefined brown sugar 8 oz (225 g)
Ground mixed spice ½ tsp (2.5 ml)
Ground nutmeg ¼ tsp (1.25ml)
Butter or margarine, melted 6 oz (175g)
Free-range eggs, beaten 3
Unrefined sugar marmalade 1 tbsp (15 ml)
Sherry 4 fl oz (100 ml)
Lemon, or orange, grated rind of ½

Thoroughly combine all the dry ingredients together in a large mixing bowl.

Add the remaining ingredients and stir well until evenly mixed. Grease two 1¾ pt (1 l) pudding basins and press half the mixture into each one.

Cut two circles of greaseproof paper about 4 in (10 cm) larger than the top of the pudding basins. Brush with oil and make a pleat in each one.

Place over the basins and secure with string. Top with a piece of kitchen roll. Steam for 6 hours.

Reheat by steaming for a further 1-1½ hours. Serve with fresh cream or custard sauce (see p. 13).

Makes 2, each serves 6
***

CARROT CAKE PUDDING WITH CINNAMON CREAM

The omission of flour in this recipe produces a
particularly light textured moist pudding.

Free-range eggs, separated 5
Unrefined brown sugar 6 oz (175 g)
Carrots, finely grated 12 oz (350 g)
Orange, grated rind of 1
Brandy or rum 1 tbsp (15 ml)
Ground almonds 12 oz (350 g)
Flaked almonds 1 oz (25 g)

CINNAMON CREAM
Natural yoghourt ⅓ pt (200 ml)
Soured cream 4 fl oz (100 ml)
Ground cinnamon 1½ tsp (7.5 ml)

Grease and base line a 9 in (23 cm) cake tin. Whisk the
egg yolks and sugar until pale and thick. Fold in the
carrots, orange rind and brandy and ground almonds.
Stiffly whisk the egg whites and fold into the carrot
mixture. Transfer to the prepared tin and level the
surface. Sprinkle with flaked almonds and bake at
325°F/170°C/gas mark 3 for about 1 hour until risen and
firm to the touch. Cool slightly then transfer to a wire
tray. Serve just warm or cold.

For the sauce: stir all the ingredients together and chill
until required.

Serves 10
***

ORANGE, PEAR & GINGER TRIFLE

Dark gingercake ½ quantity (see p. 11)
Orange liqueur 4 tbsp (60 ml)
Orange juice 4 tbsp (60 ml)
Large oranges 2
Milk 1¼ pt (750 ml)
Large ripe pears, cored & diced 2
Egg yolks 4
Unrefined brown sugar 2 oz (50 g)
Arrowroot 3 tbsp (45 ml)
Double cream, whipped ½ pt (300 ml)
Unrefined sugar crystallized ginger, sliced 1 oz (25 g)

Slice the gingercake and place in a 4 pt (2.4 l) trifle dish.
Sprinkle with the orange liqueur and orange juice. Pare
the rind from the oranges. Cut half the rind into thin
strips and place in a saucepan. Just cover with cold
water, bring to the boil. Drain and cover with cold
water. Leave to one side. Place remaining orange rind
in a saucepan with the milk. Bring just to the boil.
Remove from the heat.

Pare the white pith from the oranges using a small
serrated knife then chop the fruit into bite-size pieces.
Spoon on top of the gingercake with the diced pear.

Whisk the egg yolks, sugar and arrowroot until thick
and pale. Pour on the milk. Strain back into the pan,
then cook over gentle heat, stirring continuously until
thickened. Cool, then spoon over the fruit. Cover and
leave to go cold. Top with whipped cream. Drain and
dry the orange strips and sprinkle over the cream with
the crystallized ginger pieces.

Serves 10–12

SHERRIED SYLLABUB TRIFLE

The centre piece for a party table. To make it extra
special, decorate with fresh strawberries.

*Wholemeal sponge cake (see p. 10) ½ quantity sandwiched
together with
Unrefined sugar strawberry jam 1½ tbsp (22.5 ml)
White grape juice 3 tbsp (45 ml)
Sherry 3 tbsp + ¼ pt (195 ml)
Green grapes, halved & pipped 8 oz (225 g)
Kiwi fruit, peeled & chopped 3
Macaroons 1 quantity (see p. 9)
Lemon grated rind & juice of 1
Unrefined brown sugar 3 oz (75 g)
Double cream ½ pt (300 ml)
Flaked almonds, toasted 1 oz (25 g)*

Cut the sponge cake into small slices and arrange on the
base of a 4 pt (2.4 l) capacity trifle dish. Sprinkle with the
grape juice and 3 tbsp (45 ml) sherry. Cover with the
grapes and kiwi fruit.

Roughly break up the macaroons and sprinkle over
the fruit. Place the remaining sherry, lemon rind and
juice, sugar and cream in a bowl and whisk until thick.
Spoon over the macaroons and leave until required.
Just before serving, sprinkle with toasted almonds.

Serves 10

CHILLED MOCHA BRANDY SLICE

A rich and wicked pudding – so serve tiny slices!

Wholemeal sponge fingers 1 quantity (see p. 10)
Brandy 3 tbsp (45 ml)
Strong fresh decaffeinated coffee 4 fl oz (100 ml)
Carob bar, melted 4 oz (100 g)
Cream cheese 8 oz (225 g)
Unrefined brown sugar 2 oz (50 g)
Egg yolks 2
Walnuts, chopped 2 oz (50 g)
Double cream, whipped ¼ pt (150 ml)
Walnut halves to decorate

Base line a 2 lb (900 g) loaf tin with greaseproof or non-stick paper. Divide the sponge fingers into four equal portions. Mix the brandy and coffee together. Beat together the melted carob, cream cheese, sugar, egg yolks and chopped walnuts.

Lightly dip one portion of the sponge fingers in the coffee and arrange on the base of the tin. Spread with one third of the cream cheese mixture. Repeat the layers finishing with sponge fingers, pressing down between each layer. Cover and chill until required.

Unmould and decorate with whipped cream and walnut halves.

Serves 6–8
***

STRAWBERRY CRUNCH SURPRISE

Delicious nutty pastry holds the lemon cheese surprise
with a fresh strawberry topping.

PASTRY
Wholemeal flour 3 oz (75 g)
Ground cinnamon ½ tsp (2.5 ml)
Unrefined brown sugar 3 oz (75 g)
Hazelnuts, ground 3 oz (75 g)
Butter 4 oz (100 g)
Egg yolks 2
Vanilla essence ½ tsp (2.5 ml)
Lemon, finely grated rind of ½

FILLING
Cream cheese 6 oz (175 g)
Unrefined brown sugar 1 tbsp (15 ml)
Lemon, grated rind of ½
Strawberries 12 oz (350 g)
Unrefined sugar strawberry jam 6 tbsp (90 ml)
Lemon juice 1 tbsp (15 ml)

Mix the flour, cinnamon, sugar and hazelnuts together.
Rub in the butter, then add remaining ingredients and
work to a firm dough. Press onto base and sides of a
deep sided 8 inch (20 cm) French fluted flan tin.

Chill for 30 minutes, then bake blind at 350°F/180°C/
gas mark 4 for about 30 minutes. Leave to go cold then
remove from tin.

Mix together the cream cheese, sugar and lemon rind
and spread over base of flan. Slice or halve strawberries
and arrange attractively on top. Warm the strawberry
jam and lemon juice together. Sieve, then use to glaze
the strawberries. Chill until required.

Serves 6–8

WALNUT GATEAU

Flour-free nutty sponge layers are sandwiched together with a French butter cream to make a very special gateau.

Free-range eggs, separated 7
Unrefined brown sugar 8 oz (225 g)
Walnuts, finely chopped 11 oz (325 g)
Fresh wholemeal breadcrumbs 4 tbsp (60 ml)
Baking powder 1 tsp (5 ml)

ICING
Milk ¼ pt (150 ml)
Unrefined brown sugar 2 oz (50 g)
Egg yolks 2
Unsalted butter, softened 8 oz (225 g)
Walnuts, chopped 3 oz (75 g)

Grease and base line three 8 inch (20 cm) sandwich tins. Whisk the egg whites until stiff then whisk in half the sugar. Beat the egg yolks with the remaining sugar until thick and pale. Fold in the walnuts, breadcrumbs and baking powder. Fold in the egg whites. Divide the mixture between the prepared tins. Level the surface and bake at 375°F/190°C/gas mark 5 for about 20 minutes until just firm to the touch. Cool, then transfer to a wire tray to go cold.

Bring the milk to the boil. Beat the sugar and egg yolks until thick and pale, then pour the milk over. Stir well then return to the pan. Cook stirring all the time, over very gentle heat until lightly thickened. Strain and leave to cool. Cream the butter until light and fluffy, then beat in the custard a little at a time until creamy. Use this filling to sandwich and cover the cake completely. Sprinkle the top and sides of the cake with chopped walnuts.

Serves 12
***

CAROB TRUFFLE GATEAU

A rich truffle mixture turned into a gateau for special
occasions. Ideal to make in advance for a party.

BASE
Butter or margarine 4 oz (100 g)
Unrefined brown sugar 4 oz (100 g)
Free-range eggs, beaten 2
Self-raising wholemeal flour 3 oz (75 g)
Carob powder, sifted 1 oz (25 g)

TOPPING
Fresh ground decaffeinated coffee 2 tbsp (30 ml)
Carob bar, broken 10 oz (300 g)
Unsalted butter, diced 4 oz (100 g)
Ground almonds 4 oz (100 g)
Walnuts, chopped 2 oz (50 g)
Sultanas, chopped 2 oz (50 g)
Double cream 2 fl oz (50 ml)
Rum or brandy 2 tbsp (30 ml)
Carob powder, sifted to dust

Grease and line a 8½ in (22 cm) spring release tin.
Cream the butter and sugar together until pale and
fluffy. Beat in the eggs a little at a time, then fold in the
flour and carob powder. Spread over the base of the tin,
making a slight dip in the centre. Bake in the oven at
350°F/180°C/gas mark 4 for about 25 minutes until risen
and firm to the touch. Leave to go cold in the tin. Place
the coffee in a measuring jug and add enough boiling
water to make up to ¼ pt (150 ml). Leave to infuse for 10
minutes, then strain into a saucepan. Add the carob
and heat gently until just melted. Remove from the heat
and stir in the butter until melted, then stir in the
remaining ingredients, except carob powder. Chill until
cold, then beat well and spread over the surface of the
cake. Chill for several hours until firm to the touch.
Unmould the cake and dust lightly with carob powder.

Serves 10
***

CRANKS SACHERTORTE

A moist nutty carob cake coated with a sticky dark icing
– based on the famous Austrian torte.

Butter 4 oz (100 g)
Unrefined brown sugar 4 oz (100 g)
Free-range eggs, separated 5
Carob bar, melted 4 oz (100 g)
Ground almonds 4 oz (100 g)
Wholemeal flour 2 oz (50 g)
Unrefined sugar apricot jam, sieved 3 tbsp (45 ml)

ICING
Unrefined brown sugar 3 oz (75 g)
Carob bar 2 oz (50 g)
Carob powder 1 oz (25 g)
Water 4 tbsp (60ml)

Grease and base line an 8 in (20 cm) cake tin. Cream the
butter and sugar until pale and fluffy. Beat in the egg
yolks and then the carob. Fold in the ground almonds
and flour. Stiffly whisk the egg whites and fold in.

Transfer the mixture to the prepared tin and level the
surface. Bake at 350°F/180°C/gas mark 4 for about 45
minutes until risen and firm to the touch. Cool on a
wire tray. When cold brush the surface of the cake with
apricot jam.

Combine all the ingredients for the icing in a small
saucepan. Heat gently until dissolved then cook,
stirring frequently until the temperature reaches 220°F/
108°C on a sugar thermometer or until the icing thickly
coats the back of a wooden spoon. Cool slightly and
pour over the cake. Leave to set, then serve with
whipped cream.

Serves 8
***

COFFEE & HAZELNUT PROFITEROLES WITH CAROB SAUCE

CHOUX PASTRY
Butter 2 oz (50 g)
Water ¼ pt (150 ml)
Wholemeal flour 3 oz (75 g)
Free-range eggs, beaten 2

FILLING
Double cream ½ pt (300 ml)
Decaffeinated instant coffee powder 2 tsp (10 ml)
dissolved in boiling water 1 tbsp (15 ml)
Unrefined brown sugar 1 oz (25 g)
Hazelnuts, toasted and chopped 2 oz (50 g)

SAUCE
Carob bar broken 4 oz (100 g)
Unrefined brown sugar 2 oz (50 g)
Water ¼ pt (150 ml)
Butter 1 oz (25 g)

Place the butter and water in a saucepan and heat gently until the butter is melted, then bring to the boil. Remove from the heat and immediately beat in the flour. Beat in the egg a little at a time, until the mixture is thick. Either spoon or pipe, using a ½ in (1.5 cm) plain nozzle, 30–36 buns on to greased baking sheets. Bake at 425°F/220°C/gas mark 7 for 20–25 minutes until crisp and golden. Cool on a wire tray.

Whip the cream until 'floppy', stir in the dissolved coffee and sugar and whip again until just firm. Fold in the nuts. Split the buns and fill with the cream.

To make the sauce, place all the ingredients in a saucepan and heat gently until the carob is melted and the sugar dissolved. Simmer for 5 minutes stirring frequently. Cool slightly before serving.

Serves 6–8

CAROB CHESTNUT ROULADE

Free-range eggs 4
Unrefined brown sugar 1 oz (25 g)
Wholemeal flour ½ oz (15 g)
Carob powder, sifted ½ oz (15 g)
Ground almonds 1 oz (25 g)

FILLING
Double cream ¼ pt (150 ml)
Carob bar 4 oz (100 g)
Sweetened chestnut purée (canned) 10 oz (300 g)
Whipped cream & grated carob bar to decorate

Grease and line a 13 × 9 in (33 × 23 cm) Swiss-roll tin with non-stick paper.

Whisk the eggs and sugar in a basin over a saucepan of simmering water for about 10 minutes until really thick. Remove from the heat and whisk until cool, about 5 minutes more. (The whisk will leave a thick trail in the mixture).

Fold in the flour and carob powder, then transfer to the prepared tin. Level the surface and bake at 375°F/190°C/gas mark 5 for 10–15 minutes until risen and golden brown.

Lay a piece of greaseproof paper or a clean tea towel on the work surface and sprinkle with ground almonds. Unmould the cake on to the ground almonds. Carefully remove the paper, but leave the cake loosely covered.

For the filling heat the cream and carob together until the carob is just melted. Beat well and allow to cool. Beat in the chestnut purée and leave to go cold. Spread the filling over the surface of the cake. Starting at a short end, roll up the cake evenly like a Swiss roll. Trim the edges, and decorate, if wished with extra whipped cream and grated carob.

Serves 6
***

LEMON ROULADE

A light delicate sponge roll with a really tangy lemon flavour. Don't worry if the sponge cracks a little – it's all part of the character!

FILLING
Lemon, grated rind & juice of 1
Unrefined brown sugar 4 oz (100 g)
Butter 2 oz (50 g)
Free-range egg, beaten 1
Double cream whipped ¼ pt (150 ml)

CAKE
Free-range eggs, separated 3
Unrefined brown sugar 4 oz (100 g)
Lemon, grated rind & juice of 1
Ground almonds 3 oz (75 g)
Wholemeal flour ½ oz (15 g)

Combine the ingredients for the filling, except the cream, and place in a basin over a pan of simmering water. Cook, stirring occasionally, until thickened about 30 minutes. Chill, then fold in the cream. Grease and line a 13 × 9 in (33 × 23 cm) Swiss-roll tin with non-stick paper. Whisk the egg yolks and sugar until thick and pale. Whisk in the lemon rind and juice and whisk again until thick. Fold in the flour and 2 oz (50 g) ground almonds and transfer the mixture to the prepared tin. Level the surface and bake at 325°F/170°C/gas mark 3 for 15–20 minutes until risen and just firm to the touch.

Lay a large piece of non-stick paper on the work surface. Sprinkle with the remaining ground almonds and turn the cake out leaving the lining paper in place. Cover with a damp tea towel and leave to go cold. Remove the lining paper and trim the edges of the cake. Spread the filling over the cake and roll up from a short end.

Serves 4–6
***

INDEX

Recipes which are suitable for freezing are marked by asterisks.
***